Ethics in Early Care and Education

Nancy E. Baptiste
New Mexico State University

Luis-Vicente Reyes
New Mexico State University

Merrill
Prentice Hall

Upper Saddle River, New Jersey
Columbus, Ohio

Vice President and Publisher: Jeffery W. Johnston
Executive Editor: Ann Castel Davis
Editorial Assistant: Keli Gemrich
Production Editor: Sheryl M. Langner
Design Coordinator: Diane C. Lorenzo
Production Manager: Laura Messerly
Director of Marketing: Kevin Flanagan
Marketing Manager: Amy June
Marketing Coordinator: Barbara Koontz

---

10 9 8 7 6 5 4 3
ISBN: 0-13-092348-6

Preface

A primary concern in the field of early care and education is the need for an enhanced dialogue with preservice students and practitioners about ethics and how to expand the awareness, understanding, and application of the NAEYC (National Association for the Education of Young Children) Code of Ethical Conduct. The authors of this Student Enrichment Series text have embraced this concern because in their review of books, journals, and other resource materials for their courses, they have found that there is limited reference to the NAEYC Code of Ethical Conduct (hereafter referred to as NAEYC Code). It is only recently, through the impetus of two NAEYC publications, that early care and education courses have begun to address more comprehensively the study of the NAEYC Code. The authors, by writing *Ethics in Early Care and Education,* have created an additional resource for students, practitioners, and families to enhance their understanding of ethics in early care and education and the NAEYC Code.

There are two overarching goals that serve as the framework for the writing of *Ethics in Early Care and Education.* The first goal addresses the authors' attempt to encourage the reader to both examine the beliefs that will guide his/her ethical behavior and expand his/her knowledge, skills, and attitudes regarding ethical practice. To accomplish this, the authors focused the text on three guiding questions: How has the profession addressed the issue of professional ethics? What is the reader's relationship to the profession's core values? and How do the reader's personal and professional beliefs guide him/her in analyzing and resolving ethical dilemmas? Chapter 1 addresses the first question by examining the historical development of the NAEYC Code and reviewing its conceptual framework and content. The second question is addressed in Chapter 2 by guiding the reader to explore his/her relationship with the NAEYC Code by examining his/her personal/ professional self. The final question is addressed in Chapter 3, by providing practice opportunities in applying the NAEYC Code and a review process for analyzing and resolving ethical dilemmas.

The second overarching goal is to provide a strategy based on adult learning principles that enables readers to develop an understanding of ethics in early care and education. The major learning strategy is dialogue, or a continuous sharing of knowledge and experience as suggested by Carter and Curtis (1994) and Vella (1995). The assumptions that guide the authors' thinking about the readers' learning is that learning occurs through active engagement in reading, dialoguing and reflection (Vella, 2000). Each chapter includes activities adapted by the authors from Carter and Curtis (1994) and Vella (1995), e.g., Guiding Ideas, Achievement-Based Objectives, What I Know activities, What I Have Learned activities, and Celebrating Our Understanding. The authors hope that the activities provided throughout the chapters will encourage the reader to engage in deep self-reflection related to ethics in early care and education and the NAEYC Code.

We trust that you will find *Ethics in Early Care and Education* enjoyable reading and a contribution to the expansion of your knowledge, skills, and attitudes in early care and education ethics. We hope that this expanded knowledge will serve you well in your daily practice with young children and their families.

—Nancy Baptiste and Luis-Vicente Reyes

REFERENCES

Carter, M., & Curtis, D. (1994). *Training teachers: A harvest of theory and practice.* St. Paul, MN: Redleaf Press.

Vella, J. (1995). *Training through dialogue: Promoting effective learning with adults.* San Francisco: Jossey-Bass Publishers.

Vella, J. (2000). *Taking learning to task: Creative strategies for teaching adults.* San Francisco: Jossey-Bass Publishers.

Acknowledgments

- Lynn Hicks, Prentice Hall Publisher's Representative, who urged us to consider this project

- Ann Davis, our Merrill/Prentice Hall Editor, who graciously provided encouragement, support, and feedback

- Students enrolled in early childhood courses who read the early drafts of the book

- Members of the faculty "Publish Don't Perish" team who read and critiqued excerpts of the book

- "Publish Don't Perish" team leader, Laura Madson, who provided constructive feedback on two chapters

- Dr. Herman Garcia, head of the Department of Curriculum and Instruction, College of Education, New Mexico State University, who continuously asked "How's it going?" and provided ongoing encouragement

- Colleagues who generated excitement and energy about the book

- Steve Jeffries, Technology Fellow, who provided technical and technological assistance

- Evangeline Ward, Lilian Katz, and Stephanie Feeney for recognizing and acknowledging the importance of ethics in the early care and education profession

- Spirit Winds Coffee Shop for providing an environment conducive to our creative work

CONTENTS

Chapter 3
Using Our Understanding of the NAEYC Code and a Review
Process to Analyze and Resolve Ethical Dilemmas   45

Chapter 1

DEVELOPING AN AWARENESS OF
THE NAEYC CODE

In this chapter you will expand your understanding of the NAEYC Code by reading about its historical development and framework. "Knowing" about the history, conceptual framework, and content of the NAEYC Code will help you enlarge your personal construction about ethics in the early care and education profession. As you engage in the reading and activities, you will have an opportunity to identify what you already know about the NAEYC Code. You will also synthesize what you have learned in each section of the chapter and celebrate your understanding of the NAEYC Code. Knowledge about the NAEYC Code will help you in your journey toward discovering the profession's core values that will guide your professional practice.

GUIDING IDEAS

- Practitioners can use their exploration of the historical development of the NAEYC Code to assist them in understanding ethics in the early care and education profession.
- Practitioners, by reviewing the NAEYC Code document, can develop an initial framework for understanding the values of the early care and education profession.

ACHIEVEMENT-BASED OBJECTIVES

Through reading, engagement and reflecting, learners will have:

- Reviewed the development of the NAEYC Code from its inception to its current status.
- Examined the conceptual framework and content of the NAEYC Code.

REVIEWING THE HISTORICAL DEVELOPMENT OF THE NAEYC CODE

 **What I Know Activity**

To begin naming what you already know about ethics in the early care and education profession, please respond to the following statements:

1. What I know about ethics in the early care and education profession is...

2. What I know about the framework of the NAEYC Code is...

3. What I know about the NAEYC Code is...

     The field of early care and education, also known as early childhood education, has continuously faced the challenge of becoming a profession. One of the major challenges that the field has overcome has been the movement from an occupation to a profession. That movement is reflected in the Executive Summary of *Eager to Learn* that states "*care and education cannot be thought of as separate entities in dealing with young children*"(National Research Council and Institute of Medicine, 2000, p. 2). The emphasis on care *and* education has provided an expanded perspective in looking at the characteristics of the profession.

     Similar to other professions, the field of early care and education has embraced certain characteristics that have distinguished it as a profession such as those cited by Vander Ven (1986). From her review of the sociological literature, she listed the following elements of a profession:

*   "an established knowledge base,

- a controlled entry into the field,
- a value system around service, including a code of ethics,
- the needs of clients are defined by the profession
- autonomous practice
- a specialized education system embracing both the knowledge base and delivery skills" (Ade, Davies-Jones, & Spisak cited in Vander Ven, 1986, p. 14).

The field of early care and education, with its membership, has continued to develop the necessary professional characteristics required for a professional field.

One of the field's concentrated efforts toward professionalization was the development of formal training. The first visible effort of the profession to address formal training of its members began in 1972 with the funding of the Child Development Associate Consortium with its membership of forty-two organizations. The Consortium received $802,000 from the government to create the Child Development Associate (CDA), a program designed to credential personnel in early childhood education. The intent of this program was to provide training for personnel in preschool programs, especially in the Head Start program. The Child Development Associate is a competency-based credential that documents an individual's knowledge, skills, and attitudes that are appropriate for working with young children.

The formal CDA credentialing process developed in response to the need of a growing work force in early care and education. The number of families who needed child care services was increasing at that time due to the increased number of dual career and single parent working families. More non-parent adults, often minimally professionally prepared, came into contact with children and families on a daily basis through early care and education programs.

The regular contact of families and their children's caregivers created increased opportunities for conflicts. Conflicts included but were not limited to issues of parents' rights, children's rights, appropriate curriculum, guidance techniques, child abuse and neglect, and cultural and linguistic responsivity. Ethical dilemmas, conflicts, and questions in the field led the profession to develop a code of ethical conduct. With the increase in the number and type of conflicts, practitioners needed guidelines to address the variety of situations they were encountering in their everyday practice.

Interactions between practitioners and their "clients" can surface a variety of conflicts. The concept of ethics addresses conflicts and has historical roots in all professions. Ethics has to do with human well being and the issue of power. According to Angeles, cited in Nash (1996), ethics also has to do with examination of "ought, should, duty, right, wrong, obligation and responsibility" (p. 2). Professions that have human beings as "clients" need to assist their members in making professional judgments and in protecting their "clients." In the early care and education profession "big people" have power over "little people." The early care and education profession needs to provide safeguards for its multiple clients, children, and families.

Thus, ethics is a form of knowledge and skills practitioners can use to guide their professional behavior. Nash (1996) states that "A code of ethics embodies the highest moral ideals of the profession" (p. 96). Without a code of ethics to guide professional behavior, the profession was at a loss.

To illustrate how the profession was at a loss without a code of ethics, Luis-Vicente, one of the authors of this text, shares how he grappled with issues of what he thought was right for children and how parents sometimes disagreed. He remembers having lengthy discussions with parents regarding spanking of young children. As a program director, he did not support that type of discipline. Without a code of ethics to support his position, that of not spanking children, his work with parents was most challenging. Today, with a code of ethics as support, he would be more readily able to defend his position. The NAEYC Code provides practitioners with core values, primary responsibilities, ideals, and principles that are agreed upon by members of the profession. Practitioners can refer to a code of ethics to support their decision making and practice.

The early care and education profession began its work on a code of ethics with the challenge by Evangeline Ward in the mid-1970s to develop a draft of a code of ethics. In 1976 the NAEYC governing board agreed to develop a Code of Ethical Conduct. Lilian Katz promoted dialogue about ethics suggesting that there were some unique elements for early childhood and that it was important for the profession to have a code. According to Katz and Ward (1989), the need for the code emanated from a range of ethical problems related to: (1) power and status of practitioners, (2) multiplicity of clients, (3) ambiguity of data base, and (4) role ambiguity. The clients include children, families,

4

communities, and colleagues who represent a wide range of needs to be served. They said, "a Code of Ethical Conduct may help practitioners cope with the ambiguities with greater success" (p. 15). They also said that, "If we are further to establish ourselves as professionals, we must set high ethical and professional standards by creating conditions for the protection of children, their families and the profession" (p. 19). At the same time that the profession issued a call for the development of a code of ethics, an individual state adopted a Code of Ethical Conduct Responsibilities. The Minnesota AEYC created a code of their own with 34 principles to make sure that all early care and education professionals in the state of Minnesota had their needs addressed.

To represent the profession's needs at the national level, NAEYC, in 1984, appointed a commission to draft a code based on the work of Katz and Ward. Stephanie Feeney was appointed Chairperson and spent five years studying and drafting the Code of Ethical Conduct. Stephanie Feeney's commission studied, reflected, and dialogued in depth about the development of the Code by inviting participation from the membership of the profession to get an inclusive view of what a code of ethical conduct should look like.

The process began in 1985 with a survey distributed to its membership, through the NAEYC journal, *Young Children*. The commission received 600 responses to their survey. Of those, 331 of the responses described ethical dilemmas, and 93% of the respondents said the professional organization should immediately focus on development of the code because of the serious dilemmas and "ethical pain" experienced by practitioners as described by Kipnis (Feeney & Freeman, 1999). The second step involved conducting ethics workshops throughout the country. The focus of the workshops was "What should the 'good early childhood educator' do when . . . " The third step was to publish ethical dilemmas in *Young Children* and solicit responses from the membership. The fourth step was to actually draft a code that was presented at a November 1988 conference. The actual code, entitled the NAEYC Code of Ethical Conduct, was approved by the NAEYC Board in 1989 and published in *Young Children* in November 1989. The code has been described by Feeney and Freeman (1999) as "a living document, designed to be responsive to changes in the Association's membership, the moral climate of our society, and new challenges faced by the profession" (pp. 17–18). To assure that the document is dynamic, the code is reviewed and revised every five years.

In addition to the Code, the profession developed a statement of commitment. The purpose of the commitment statement is to recognize that the only way the NAEYC Code can continue being a viable professional document is for each practitioner to adhere to the Code in order to further the values of the early care and education profession. The development of the NAEYC Code was inclusive of many people from its membership. The profession recognizes the work done by Feeney and others as a hallmark of the profession.

Now that we have learned about the historical development of the NAEYC Code, it is time to synthesize our learning by responding to reflective questions. While you are completing the What I Have Learned activity, we will begin preparation for a discussion about the document description, conceptual framework, and contents of the NAEYC Code.

What I Have Learned

Reflective Questions

If you are in a classroom setting, "Think, Pair, and Share" (Wolfe, 2000). Think about your response to the question, find a partner, and share your responses. If you are not in a classroom setting share your thinking with a friend.

1. How would you describe the development of the NAEYC Code?
2. What was most exciting to you about the development of the NAEYC Code?
3. Why do you think it is important that the NAEYC membership participated in the development of a Code of Ethical Conduct?
4. What process would you develop for including the diverse members of the early care and education profession (practitioners, administrators, students, etc.) in the next revision of the NAEYC Code?

"WALKING THROUGH" THE CONCEPTUAL FRAMEWORK AND CONTENT OF THE NAEYC CODE OF ETHICAL CONDUCT

 **What I Know Activity**

The NAEYC Code consists of core values, ideals, and principles. Please read the following examples and respond to the questions.
Examples:

■ Respecting the dignity, worth, and uniqueness of each individual (child, family member, and colleague).
1. What name would you give to this example from the NAEYC Code?

_____

■ I-1.1 To be familiar with the knowledge base of early childhood care and education and to keep current through continuing education and in-service training.
2. What name would you give to this example from the NAEYC Code?

_____

■ P-1.1 Above all, **we shall not harm children**. We shall not participate in practices that are disrespectful, degrading, dangerous, exploitative, intimidating, emotionally damaging, or physically harmful to children. This principle has precedence over all others in this Code.
3. What name would you give to this example from the NAEYC Code?

_____

In this section of Chapter 1, we will discuss the conceptual framework and contents of the NAEYC Code. We encourage you, the reader, to thoroughly review and refer throughout the chapter to the NAEYC Code document at the end of this chapter. Let us remind ourselves of what a code of ethics is. Clyde and Rodd (1989) state that "A code of ethics, is a set of value judgments relating to the way in which the person or group should behave in order to uphold or abide by the professional values of that group . . ." (p. 2). We will start by examining the Preamble. We will then look at the core values, primary responsibilities, ideals, and principles of the NAEYC Code. These five aspects of the document comprise the conceptual framework and contents of the Code.

The preamble, the first part of the document, sets the tone for the NAEYC Code. The preamble says that the Code is primarily for practitioners who work on a daily basis with children rather than people who do not work directly with children such as program administrators and college professors. The preamble also serves to remind us that the Code applies to practitioners serving children from birth through age eight in a variety of early care and education settings to include but not be limited to preschools, child care centers, family child care homes, Head Start programs, kindergartens, and primary classrooms up to third grade.

Next, let us look at the core values in the NAEYC Code. The purpose of the core values is to establish the profession's idea of what values are worthwhile as they relate to professional behavior. The core values represent what early care and education professionals are committed to and stem from values that have developed historically in the field. Core values are not material things; they are abstract ideas, such as appreciation and recognition. The six core values are: (1) appreciating childhood as a unique developmental stage; (2) basing our work on knowledge of child development; (3) appreciating and supporting the close ties between the child and family; (4) recognizing that children are best understood in the context of family, culture, community, and society; (5) respecting the dignity, worth, and uniqueness of each individual; and (6) helping children and families reach their full potential.

The core values provide a disposition for our thinking about how we need to behave on a daily basis and help us to understand the conceptual framework of the code. For example, one of the core values is recognizing that children are best understood and supported in the context of family, culture, community, and society. To demonstrate how that core value will guide the teacher, we will look at curriculum planning. When the teacher is developing curriculum for young children, he or she will involve families in the planning, always keeping in mind the children's language, culture, and home and including responsive activities. He or she will then be supporting one of the profession's core values.

The next section of the Code, the conceptual framework, further reminds us of the "clients" of the early care and education profession. The code says there are four groups of people to whom early care and education practitioners have responsibilities: (1) children, (2) families, (3) colleagues, and (4) community members. In our profession, because we deal with dependent children, we must always have "other adults" in mind. Children require adults (parents, other family members, early care and education practitioners, and individuals in the community) to meet their needs. As we look at the conceptual framework of the Code, we see that in each section there is a description of ethical responsibilities, related Ideals, and a description of principles.

To begin with, let us examine the Code's primary responsibilities to children, families, colleagues, community, and society. The Code defines these responsibilities as professional relationships that practitioners have with the selected four groups. The ethical responsibilities provide us with the framework for thinking about the ideals.

Perhaps the best way to think about the ideals of the Code is in terms of "how we should behave." Practitioners can use the ideals as signposts of expected behavior that supports their professional responsibilities to children, families, colleagues, and community and society. The Code provides in each section a set of ideals. What is important to know is that ideals represent those behaviors that the profession expects its practitioners to demonstrate. For example, ideal I-1.1 states "to be familiar with the knowledge base of early childhood care and education and to keep current through continuing education and in-service training." How the practitioner can utilize this ideal to guide his/her behavior is by becoming aware of and participating in community training and state, regional, and national conferences.

Following the ideals in each section of the Code are principles. The principles might best be thought of as "right thinking." Principles are compelling guides for an active conscience. We always need to stay alert and reflect on our practice as we relate to others. For example, principle P-1.1 appears in bold type, and necessarily so: *Above all, we shall not harm children.* The Code says that this principle has

9

shall not harm children. The Code says that this principle has precedence over all other principles. This principle serves as a directive to practitioners to remind them of their responsibility to children. This principle tells practitioners in no uncertain terms that they may not harm children physically, emotionally, sexually, or in any other way. The concept of harm really needs to be examined. Years ago, people readily spanked their children without awareness of the harm this can cause to children. Now with advanced research we know that spanking is not appropriate as a guidance technique because it can cause both physical and psychological harm to children.

The development of the NAEYC Code is a hallmark in our profession. It has provided practitioners with a set of values, responsibilities, ideals, and principles that guide professional behavior. Nancy, one of the authors of this text, says that every time she reads the NAEYC Code, she is reminded as to how important it is that everyone in the field be aware of the Code, know it, use it, and critique it. She especially likes the statement of commitment at the end. The statement says, "As an individual who works with young children, I commit myself to furthering the values of early childhood education as they are reflected in the NAEYC Code, and then lists commitment actions. Luis-Vicente, on the other hand, said that every time he reads the NAEYC statement of commitment, which he has many times during his career, he has been motivated to work toward adhering to the NAEYC Code. For example, the commitment statement says, "Be open to new ideas and be willing to learn from the suggestions of others." He says that this statement causes him to continuously renew and refocus his practice.

The authors believe that ethics education workshops should be part of all training events to ensure that the profession revisits the NAEYC Code. It will soon be time to revise the NAEYC Code. The revision committee will need to hear the voices of the profession to ensure that the Code remains a dynamic document.

We invite you now to synthesize your learning by responding to the reflective questions provided in the What I Have Learned activity. While you are reflecting on your learning, we will begin to prepare for our next chapter.

What I Have Learned

| Reflective Questions |

Reflective Questions

If you are in a classroom setting, "Think, Pair, and Share." Think about your response to the question, find a partner, and share your responses. If you are not in a classroom setting, share your thinking with a friend.

1. What have you learned about the conceptual framework and content of the NAEYC Code?
2. What is your response to learning about the NAEYC Code?
3. Why do you think it is important to thoroughly study the NAEYC Code?
4. What might be some changes you would make to the NAEYC Code?

CELEBRATING OUR UNDERSTANDING

In the first section in Chapter 1, you learned about the historical development of the NAEYC Code. In the second section you examined the conceptual framework and content of the NAEYC Code. What is exciting to know is that you have expanded your construction of early care and education professionalism to include the language of ethics. It is important for practitioners to have this knowledge as a tool to guide professional decisions that need to be made on a daily basis.

Give yourself a pat on the back for completing this chapter and join us in the next chapter where you will begin to move from an awareness level to a deeper understanding of the NAEYC Code.

REFERENCES AND RESOURCES

Bredekamp, S., & Copple, C. (1997). (Eds.). *Developmentally appropriate practice in early childhood programs* (Rev. ed.). Washington, DC: NAEYC.

Carter, M., & Curtis, D. (1994*). Training teachers: A harvest of theory and practice*. St. Paul, MN: Redleaf Press.

Clyde, M., & Rodd, J. (1989). Professional ethics: There's more to it than meets the eye. *Early Child Development and Care, 53*, 1–12.

Feeney, S. & Chun. R. (1985). Effective teachers of young children. *Young Children, 41*(1), 47–52.

Feeney, S., & Freeman, N. (1999). *Ethics and the early childhood educator: Using the NAEYC Code.* Washington, DC: NAEYC.

Feeney, S., Freeman, N. K., & Moravcik, E. (2000). *Teaching the NAEYC code of ethical conduct*. Activity sourcebook. [Companion resource to ethics and the early childhood educator: Using the NAEYC code]. Washington, DC: NAEYC.

Feeney, S. & Kipnis (1985). Professional ethics in early childhood education. *Young Children, 40*(3), 54–58.

Katz, L. G. (1995). *Talks with teachers of young children: A collection.* Norwood, NJ: Ablex.

Katz, L. G., & Ward, E. (1989*). Ethical behavior in early childhood education.* Expanded Edition. Washington, DC: NAEYC

Katz, L. G., & Ward, E. (1978). *Ethical behavior in early childhood education.* Washington, DC: NAEYC.

Nash, R. (1996). *"Real world" ethics: frameworks for educators and human service professionals.* New York: Teachers College Press.

National Research Council and Institute of Medicine (2000). *Eager to learn: educating our preschoolers.* Committee on early childhood pedagogy. Barbara Bowman, M. Suzanne Donovan & Susan Burns (Eds.) Commission on Behavioral and Social Sciences and Education. Washington, DC: National Academy Press.

Vander Ven K. (1986). And you have a ways to go: The current status and emerging issues in training and education for child care practice. In K. Vander Ven & E. Tittnich (Eds.), *Competent caregiver— competent children: Training and education for child care practice* (pp. 13–34). New York: Haworth Press.

Vella, J. (1995). *Training through dialogue: Promoting effective learning with adults.* San Francisco: Jossey-Bass Publishers.

Wolfe, B. (2000). "Cooperative learning in the college classroom," Workshop at New Scripts Institute, North Carolina.

Adopted 1989
Amended 1997

Code of Ethical Conduct

Preamble

NAEYC recognizes that many daily decisions required of those who work with young children are of a moral and ethical nature. The NAEYC Code of Ethical Conduct offers guidelines for responsible behavior and sets forth a common basis for resolving the principal ethical dilemmas encountered in early childhood care and education. The primary focus is on daily practice with children and their families in programs for children from birth through 8 years of age, such as infant/toddler programs, preschools, child care centers, family child care homes, kindergartens, and primary classrooms. Many of the provisions also apply to specialists who do not work directly with children, including program administrators, parent and vocational educators, college professors, and child care licensing specialists.

Core Values

Standards of ethical behavior in early childhood care and education are based on commitment to core values that are deeply rooted in the history of our field. We have committed ourselves to

- Appreciating childhood as a unique and valuable stage of the human life cycle
- Basing our work with children on knowledge of child development
- Appreciating and supporting the close ties

between the child and family
- Recognizing that children are best understood and supported in the context of family, culture, community, and society
- Respecting the dignity, worth, and uniqueness of each individual (child, family member, and colleague)
- Helping children and adults achieve their full potential in the context of relationships that are based on trust, respect, and positive regard

Conceptual Framework

The Code sets forth a conception of our professional responsibilities in four sections, each addressing an arena of professional relationships: (1) children, (2) families, (3) colleagues, and (4) community and society. Each section includes an introduction to the primary responsibilities of the early childhood practitioner in that arena, a set of ideals pointing in the direction of exemplary professional practice, and a set of principles defining practices that are required, prohibited, and permitted.

The ideals reflect the aspirations of practitioners. **The principles** are intended to guide conduct and assist practitioners in resolving ethical dilemmas encountered in the field. There is not necessarily a corresponding principle for each ideal. Both ideals and principles are intended to direct practitioners to those questions which, when responsibly answered, will provide the basis for conscientious decisionmaking. While the Code provides specific direction and suggestions for addressing some ethical dilemmas, many others will require the practitioner to combine the guidance of the Code with sound professional judgment.

The ideals and principles in this Code present a shared

conception of professional responsibility that affirms our commitment to the core values of our field. The Code publicly acknowledges the responsibilities that we in the field have assumed and in so doing supports ethical behavior in our work. Practitioners who face ethical dilemmas are urged to seek guidance in the applicable parts of this Code and in the spirit that informs the whole.

Ethical dilemmas always exist

Often, "the right answer" -- the best ethical course of action to take?is not obvious. There may be no readily apparent, positive way to handle a situation. One important value may contradict another. When we are caught "on the horns of a dilemma," it is our professional responsibility to consult with all relevant parties in seeking the most ethical course of action to take.

Section I: Ethical responsibilities to children

Childhood is a unique and valuable stage in the life cycle. Our paramount responsibility is to provide safe, healthy, nurturing, and responsive settings for children. We are committed to support children's development, respect individual differences, help children learn to live and work cooperatively, and promote health, self-awareness, competence, self-worth, and resiliency.

Ideals

I-1.1. To be familiar with the knowledge base of early childhood care and education and to keep current through continuing education and in-service training.

I-1.2. To base program practices upon current knowledge in the field of child development and related disciplines and upon particular knowledge of each child.

I-1.3. To recognize and respect the uniqueness and the potential of each child.

I-1.4. To appreciate the special vulnerability of children.

I-1.5. To create and maintain safe and healthy settings that foster children's social, emotional, intellectual, and physical development and that respect their dignity and their contributions.

I-1.6. To support the right of each child to play and learn in inclusive early childhood programs to the fullest extent consistent with the best interests of all involved. As with adults who are disabled in the larger community, children with disabilities are ideally served in the same settings in which they would participate if they did not have a disability.

I-1.7. To ensure that children with disabilities have access to appropriate and convenient support services and to advocate for the resources necessary to provide the most appropriate settings for all children.

Principles

P-1.1. Above all, we shall not harm children. We shall not participate in practices that are disrespectful, degrading, dangerous, exploitative, intimidating, emotionally damaging, or physically harmful to children. This principle has precedence over all others in this Code.

P-1.2. We shall not participate in practices that discriminate against children by denying benefits, giving special advantages, or excluding them from programs or activities on the basis of their race, ethnicity, religion, sex, national origin, language, ability, or the status, behavior, or beliefs of their parents. (This principle does not apply to programs that have a lawful mandate to provide services to a particular population of children.)

P-1.3. We shall involve all of those with relevant knowledge (including staff and parents) in decisions concerning a child.

P-1.4. For every child we shall implement adaptations in teaching strategies, learning environment, and curricula, consult with the family, and seek recommendations from appropriate specialists to maximize the potential of the child to benefit from the program. If, after these efforts have been made to work with a child and family, the child does not appear to be benefiting from a program, or the child is seriously jeopardizing the ability of other children to benefit from the program, we shall communicate with the family and appropriate specialists to determine the child's current needs; identify the setting and services most suited to meeting these needs; and assist the family in placing the child in an appropriate setting.

P-1.5. We shall be familiar with the symptoms of child abuse, including physical, sexual, verbal, and emotional abuse, and neglect. We shall know and follow state laws and community procedures that protect children against abuse and neglect.

P-1.6. When we have reasonable cause to suspect child abuse or neglect, we shall report it to the appropriate community agency and follow up to ensure that

18

appropriate action has been taken. When appropriate, parents or guardians will be informed that the referral has been made.

P-1.7. When another person tells us of a suspicion that a child is being abused or neglected, we shall assist that person in taking appropriate action to protect the child.

P-1.8. When a child protective agency fails to provide adequate protection for abused or neglected children, we acknowledge a collective ethical responsibility to work toward improvement of these services.

P-1.9. When we become aware of a practice or situation that endangers the health or safety of children, but has not been previously known to do so, we have an ethical responsibility to inform those who can remedy the situation and who can protect children from similar danger.

Section II: Ethical responsibilities to families

Families are of primary importance in children's development. (The term family may include others, besides parents, who are responsibly involved with the child.) Because the family and the early childhood practitioner have a common interest in the child's welfare, we acknowledge a primary responsibility to bring about collaboration between the home and school in ways that enhance the child's development.

Ideals

I-2.1. To develop relationships of mutual trust with families we serve.

I-2.2. To acknowledge and build upon strengths and competencies as we support families in their task of nurturing children.

I-2.3. To respect the dignity of each family and its culture, language, customs, and beliefs.

I-2.4. To respect families' childrearing values and their right to make decisions for their children.

I-2.5. To interpret each child's progress to parents within the framework of a developmental perspective and to help families understand and appreciate the value of developmentally appropriate early childhood practices.

I-2.6. To help family members improve their understanding of their children and to enhance their skills as parents.

I-2.7. To participate in building support networks for families by providing them with opportunities to interact with program staff, other families, community resources, and professional services.

Principles

P-2.1.We shall not deny family members access to their child's classroom or program setting.

P-2.2. We shall inform families of program philosophy, policies, and personnel qualifications, and explain why we teach as we do?which should be in accordance with our ethical responsibilities to children (see Section I).

P-2.3. We shall inform families of and when appropriate, involve them in policy decisions.

P-2.4. We shall involve families in significant decisions affecting their child.

P-2.5. We shall inform the family of accidents involving their child, of risks such as exposures to contagious disease that may result in infection, and of occurrences that might result in emotional stress.

P-2.6. To improve the quality of early childhood care and education, we shall cooperate with qualified child development researchers. Families shall be fully informed of any proposed research projects involving their children and shall have the opportunity to give or withhold consent without penalty. We shall not permit or participate in research that could in any way hinder the education, development, or well-being of children.

P-2.7. We shall not engage in or support exploitation of families. We shall not use our relationship with a family for private advantage or personal gain, or enter into relationships with family members that might impair our effectiveness in working with children.

P-2.8. We shall develop written policies for the protection of confidentiality and the disclosure of children's records. These policy documents shall be made available to all program personnel and families. Disclosure of children's records beyond family members, program personnel, and consultants having an obligation of confidentiality shall require familial consent (except in cases of abuse or neglect).

P-2.9. We shall maintain confidentiality and shall respect the family's right to privacy, refraining from disclosure of confidential information and intrusion into family life. However, when we have reason to believe that a child's welfare is at risk, it is permissible to share confidential information with agencies and individuals who may be able to intervene in the child's interest.

P-2.10. In cases where family members are in conflict, we shall work openly, sharing our observations of the child, to help all parties involved make informed decisions. We shall refrain from becoming an advocate for one party.

P-2.11. We shall be familiar with and appropriately use community resources and professional services that support families. After a referral has been made, we shall follow up to ensure that services have been appropriately provided.

Section III. Ethical responsibilities to colleagues

In a caring, cooperative work place, human dignity is respected, professional satisfaction is promoted, and positive relationships are modeled. Based upon our core values, our primary responsibility in this arena is to establish and maintain settings and relationships that support productive work and meet professional needs. The same ideals that apply to children are inherent in our responsibilities to adults.

A. Responsibilities to co-workers

Ideals

I-3A.1. To establish and maintain relationships of respect, trust, and cooperation with co-workers.

I-3A.2. To share resources and information with co-workers.

I-3A.3. To support co-workers in meeting their professional needs and in their professional development.

P-3A.4. To accord co-workers due recognition of professional achievement.

Principles

P-3A.1. When we have concern about the professional behavior of a co-worker, we shall first let that person know of our concern, in a way that shows respect for personal dignity and for the diversity to be found among staff members, and then attempt to resolve the matter collegially.

P-3A.2. We shall exercise care in expressing views regarding the personal attributes or professional conduct of co-workers. Statements should be based on firsthand knowledge and relevant to the interests of children and programs.

B. Responsibilities to employers

Ideals

I-3B.1. To assist the program in providing the highest quality of service.

I-3B.2. To do nothing that diminishes the reputation of the program in which we work unless it is violating laws and regulations designed to protect children or the provisions of this Code.

Principles

P-3B.1. When we do not agree with program policies, we shall first attempt to effect change through constructive action within the organization.

P-3B.2. We shall speak or act on behalf of an organization only when authorized. We shall take care to acknowledge when we are speaking for the organization and when we are expressing a personal judgment.

P-3B.3. We shall not violate laws or regulations designed to protect children and shall take appropriate action consistent with this Code when aware of such violations.

C. Responsibilities to employees

Ideals

I-3C.1. To promote policies and working conditions that foster mutual respect, competence, well-being, and positive self-esteem in staff members.

I-3C.2. To create a climate of trust and candor that will enable staff to speak and act in the best interests of children, families, and the field of early childhood care and education.

I-3C.3. To strive to secure equitable compensation (salary and benefits) for those who work with or on behalf of young children.

Principles

P-3C.1. In decisions concerning children and programs, we shall appropriatcly utilize the education, training, experience, and expertise of staff members.

P-3C.2. We shall provide staff members with safe and supportive working conditions that permit them to carry out their responsibilities, timely and nonthreatening evaluation procedures, written grievance procedures, constructive feedback, and opportunities for continuing professional development and advancement.

P-3C.3. We shall develop and maintain comprehensive written personnel policies that define program standards and, when applicable, that specify the extent to which employees are accountable for their conduct outside the work place. These policies shall be given to new staff members and shall be available for review by all staff members.

P-3C.4. Employees who do not meet program standards shall be informed of areas of concern and, when possible, assisted in improving their performance.

P-3C.5. Employees who are dismissed shall be informed of the reasons for their termination. When a dismissal is for cause, justification must be based on evidence of inadequate or inappropriate behavior that is accurately documented, current, and available for the employee to review.

P-3C.6. In making evaluations and recommendations, judgments shall be based on fact and relevant to the interests of children and programs.

P-3C.7. Hiring and promotion shall be based solely on a person's record of accomplishment and ability to carry out the responsibilities of the position.

P-3C.8. In hiring, promotion, and provision of training,

we shall not participate in any form of discrimination based on race, ethnicity, religion, gender, national origin, culture, disability, age, or sexual preference. We shall be familiar with and observe laws and regulations that pertain to employment discrimination.

Section IV: Ethical responsibilities to community and society

Early childhood programs operate within a context of an immediate community made up of families and other institutions concerned with children's welfare. Our responsibilities to the community are to provide programs that meet its needs, to cooperate with agencies and professions that share responsibility for children, and to develop needed programs that are not currently available. Because the larger society has a measure of responsibility for the welfare and protection of children, and because of our specialized expertise in child development, we acknowledge an obligation to serve as a voice for children everywhere.

Ideals

I.4.1. To provide the community with high-quality (age and individually appropriate, and culturally and socially sensitive) education/care programs and services.

I-4.2. To promote cooperation among agencies and interdisciplinary collaboration among professions concerned with the welfare of young children, their families, and their teachers.

I-4.3. To work, through education, research, and advocacy, toward an environmentally safe world in which all children receive adequate health care, food, and shelter, are nurtured, and live free from violence.

I-4.4. To work, through education, research, and advocacy, toward a society in which all young children have access to high-quality education/care programs.

I-4.5. To promote knowledge and understanding of young children and their needs. To work toward greater social acknowledgment of children's rights and greater social acceptance of responsibility for their well-being.

I-4.6. To support policies and laws that promote the well-being of children and families, and to oppose those that impair their well-being. To participate in developing policies and laws that are needed, and to cooperate with other individuals and groups in these efforts.

I-4.7. To further the professional development of the field of early childhood care and education and to strengthen its commitment to realizing its core values as reflected in this Code.

Principles

P-4.1. We shall communicate openly and truthfully about the nature and extent of services that we provide.

P-4.2. We shall not accept or continue to work in positions for which we are personally unsuited or professionally unqualified. We shall not offer services that we do not have the competence, qualifications, or resources to provide.

P-4.3. We shall be objective and accurate in reporting the knowledge upon which we base our program practices.

P-4.4. We shall cooperate with other professionals who work with children and their families.

P-4.5. We shall not hire or recommend for employment any person whose competence, qualifications, or character makes him or her unsuited for the position.

P-4.6. We shall report the unethical or incompetent behavior of a colleague to a supervisor when informal resolution is not effective.

P-4.7. We shall be familiar with laws and regulations that serve to protect the children in our programs.

P-4.8. We shall not participate in practices which are in violation of laws and regulations that protect the children in our programs.

P-4.9. When we have evidence that an early childhood program is violating laws or regulations protecting children, we shall report it to persons responsible for the program. If compliance is not accomplished within a reasonable time, we will report the violation to appropriate authorities who can be expected to remedy the situation.

P-4.10. When we have evidence that an agency or a professional charged with providing services to children, families, or teachers is failing to meet its obligations, we acknowledge a collective ethical responsibility to report the problem to appropriate authorities or to the public.

P-4.11. When a program violates or requires its employees to violate this Code, it is permissible, after fair assessment of the evidence, to disclose the identity of that program.

Statement of commitment

As an individual who works with young children, I commit myself to furthering the values of early childhood education as they are reflected in the NAEYC Code of Ethical Conduct.

To the best of my ability I will

- Ensure that programs for young children are based on current knowledge of child development and early childhood education.
- Respect and support families in their task of nurturing children.
- Respect colleagues in early childhood education and support them in maintaining the NAEYC Code of Ethical Conduct.
- Serve as an advocate for children, their families, and their teachers in community and society.
- Maintain high standards of professional conduct.
- Recognize how personal values, opinions, and biases can affect professional judgment.
- Be open to new ideas and be willing to learn from the suggestions of others.
- Continue to learn, grow, and contribute as a professional.
- Honor the ideals and principles of the NAEYC Code of Ethical Conduct.

This document is an official position statement of the National Association for the Education of Young Children.

This statement may be purchased as a brochure, and the Statement of Commitment is available as a poster suitable for framing. See our catalog for ordering information.

Chapter 2

MOVING FROM AN AWARENESS LEVEL TO A DEEPER UNDERSTANDING OF THE NAEYC CODE

In this chapter you will explore the relationship of your personal/professional values to the ethics of the early care and education profession as expressed in the NAEYC Code. As you engage in the reading and activities, you will identify what you already know about the concept of personal/professional self. You will also have an opportunity to learn about two tools, dialogue and reflection. The tools of dialogue and reflection can assist you when your personal/professional values, beliefs, and experiences conflict with the NAEYC Code. Additionally, you will synthesize what you have learned in each section of the chapter and celebrate your deeper understanding of the NAEYC Code. By enhancing your understanding of your personal/professional values and their relationship to the profession's core values through dialogue and reflection, you will move to a deeper understanding of the NAEYC Code.

GUIDING IDEAS

- Practitioners enhance their learning about the NAEYC Code by examining the relationship between their personal/ professional self and the core values of the NAEYC Code.
- Practitioners can use the tools of dialogue and reflection to assist them when conflicts occur between their personal/professional values, beliefs, and experiences and the core values of the NAEYC Code.

ACHIEVEMENT-BASED OBJECTIVES

Through reading, engagement, and reflection, learners will have:

- Analyzed the concept of personal/ professional self and its relationship to the NAEYC Code.

31

- Examined and practiced the use of two tools, dialogue and reflection, for gaining a deeper understanding of coping with conflict between personal/professional values and the core values in the NAEYC Code.

EXPLORING THE CONCEPTS OF PERSONAL SELF AND PROFESSIONAL SELF

 **What I Know Activity**

Please read the following scenarios and respond to the questions.

Clara, a 24-year-old preschool teacher assistant, observes Thomas and Jonathan fighting over the yellow dump truck. Each child is trying to pull the truck away from the other. Clara knows that an NAEYC Code value is "appreciating childhood as a unique and valuable stage of the human life cycle." That value supports the principle "We shall not harm children" (P-1.1). With that knowledge, Clara redirects Thomas to play with the green dump truck.

Clara has two children of her own, ages three and five. After a long day of working with the children of other families, she observes her daughter and son fighting over a bag of Goldfish crackers. Without hesitation she grabs the bag of Goldfish crackers and immediately spanks both children for fighting.

1. Describe Clara's professional values as expressed in the scenarios.
2. Describe Clara's personal values as expressed in the scenarios.
3. Describe how Clara's personal and professional values conflict.
4. Recall a situation when your personal and professional values conflicted.

Early childhood practitioners benefit professionally from exploring the concept of the personal/ professional self. This exploration provides the practitioner with understanding that assists him or her in resolving conflicts between personal/professional self values and the NAEYC Code values. Often the exploration begins with the questions "Who am I?" and "Why do I have the values and beliefs that I do?" These questions, which relate to one's personal self, are questions that require responses when we are studying ethics in the early care and education profession.

We will begin by examining the concept of personal self. The personal self is that part of each of us that holds our values and beliefs, helps explain who we are, and guides our behavior. A man named Pierre Bourdieu has given much thought to the development of the personal self. Bourdieu, born in France, gives us the idea of *habitus* to understand the personal self (Bourdieu & Passeron, 1991). What he says is that through the process of living, people acquire certain ways of knowing, values, and behaviors. For example, have you ever asked yourself why some people believe that brushing their teeth before showering is better than brushing their teeth after showering? Bourdieu would say that there were models for either of those choices in the individual's home.

We know that what we see and hear in our interactions in our families, neighborhoods, communities, social organizations, and society provide models for behavior and influence our developing values, which become part of our personal selves. Bourdieu has described the process of being influenced by other's beliefs, values and behaviors as *inculcation*. The majority of our values come from our homes, neighborhoods, communities, and society. Values are what guide the behaviors that have emerged from our individual context. Those values and beliefs that we internalize then guide our behavior.

Let us use the example of Clara in the scenario of her home to illustrate the concept of inculcation. We can say that Clara's personal self includes models and values of guidance that support spanking of young children. Those models and values may have come from her home, her religion, or her culture. She might also tell you that she believes in spanking and that she values spanking as an appropriate guidance tool because her parents used spanking as a guidance tool. She might tell you that she believes inappropriate behavior must be responded to immediately with physical intervention. That is a belief and value that she has internalized through the process of inculcation. Her home, religion, community, and culture support this value. The personal self comes "to be" through the process of *inculcation* as we interact with others and things in our environment. This is a continuing lifetime process. For example, when Clara married, the home she and her husband created brought together two worlds of values and beliefs, perhaps some similar, perhaps some different. As their relationship emerged, their personal selves adjusted to any differences in values and beliefs. Thus, the personal self engages in many adjustments throughout the lifespan.

As we were writing, some of our own models and values came to mind. Luis-Vicente said that boys in his family played with toys and materials that were designed for "male" play; for example, boys played with trucks and tools. When asked why that was the case, he said, "It was not O.K. by the values and beliefs of my home and community for boys to play with dolls and gender specific dress up clothes. I had been *inculcated* by my home and community values to see specific role definitions for male and female child play." Nancy, on the other hand, believes that children regardless of gender should play with all types of toys and materials. Both her sons and daughter had their own dolls and trucks. When asked how she had come to that decision, she responded, "In my family although there was role differentiation between my mother and father, they did not impose limitations on the behavior of their two daughters. My sister and I were encouraged to engage in diverse activities both indoors and outdoors, for example, yard maintenance, snow shoveling, fishing, rather than gender specified activities. As I look back, I guess I was *inculcated* with values of gender equity." As we have seen in the above examples, the inculcation of family values influences personal values.

As we examine the inculcation process for our professional values, we realize that as adults many of our values are influenced by our professional experience and career preparation. Let us now look at the development of the professional self. The professional self emerges similarly to the personal self. The field of early care and education has continuously been engaged in the process of professionalization, that is, becoming a recognized, valued profession in our society. We know that the NAEYC Code's core values come from a collective effort of early care and education professionals throughout the country. This group, through consensus building, has offered a set of values to guide professional behavior acceptable to its professional membership. Clara did not spank the fighting children in her child care setting because she has been inculcated with professional values. The NAEYC Code is presented to students enrolled in professional preparation programs or through in-service staff development. In the process of professional development, students are being inculcated with a specified set of professional values to guide their behavior. The enforcement of these values lies within the profession itself, for example, a child care center setting in which the program director inculcates the staff with the professional values as expressed in the NAEYC Code. The director then monitors staff to ensure that the code guides their behavior. As we can see then, the professional self is created similarly to the personal self through the inculcation process. In this process, it is the profession that creates and supports the values.

Let us now revisit the scenario of Clara in her interactions with children in the center setting. We know that Clara believes that in her home, spanking is an effective guidance tool. Spanking makes sense to her based on personal values. On the other hand, she adheres very closely to her professional code of ethics in her employment setting as evidenced by her use of redirection rather than spanking the children fighting over the same toy. The authors think that Clara's diverse behavior in two different settings demonstrates a conflict of her personal and professional values as reflected by the profession's core values. Clara's behavior suggests a fragmented personal/professional self. What supports Clara's fragmentation is that there are setting-specific values that guide Clara's behavior, that is, home values, which guide personal behavior at home, and the core values of the NAEYC Code, which guide Clara's behavior in her work setting. This conflict exists because Clara has not dialogued and reflected on why she behaves differently in the two settings. The conflict is detrimental to Clara as an early childhood practitioner because she is not aware of the discrepancy between her personal and professional self. She doesn't know that she doesn't know. When you know that you understand the discrepancy between values of your personal self and your professional self, and the NAEYC Code values, then you can exercise appropriate professional judgment.

Join us now in a conversation about how practitioners can use the tools of dialogue and reflection to reconcile their conflicts between personal/professional self and the NAEYC Code. While we are preparing for the discussion, you can be reflecting on the following questions.

What I Have Learned

Reflective Questions

If you are in a classroom setting, "Think, Pair, and Share." Think about your response to the question/statement, find a partner, and share your responses. If you are not in a classroom setting, share your thinking with a friend.

1. Identify two personal and two professional values you have. Briefly describe where you think they came from.
2. What is your feeling about having personal and professional conflicts?
3. Compare the NAEYC Code core values with your own personal values. Note where there is agreement and conflict.
4. How would you reconcile a conflict between a personal and professional value?

EXAMINING AND PRACTICING DIALOGUE AND REFLECTION

What I Know Activity

Dialogue occurs when individuals come together to have a conversation about an issue or topic. According to Vella (1995), "Dialogue assumes two human beings as subjects of their own learning, and sharing research data, experience, and questions to transform both their own learning and the very knowledge they are examining" (p. 162). Dialogue differs from conversation in that dialogue requires that individuals not only engage in the conversation but also think about what has influenced their world view, that is, how home, community, education, experience, and culture have influenced their thinking, values and behavior. For example, Rosemarie and Julia engaged in dialogue about the best way to observe young children. They talked about the importance of observation and how and where they learned observation skills.

1. Describe a time when you engaged in a dialogue about an issue related to early care and education.

Reflection occurs when an individual examines his/her own assumptions, experiences, values, and attitudes in relationship to a behavior, thought, or practice (Brookfield, 1995). In this reflective process, self-examination moves one to take action. For example, after holding an infant in her arms for fifteen minutes, Suzanne reflected on this experience. What she learned was that the infant she held gave her many cues (e.g., grimacing, wiggling, crying) that told her that she needed to reexamine her behavior. She changed the position of the infant and noted that the infant was now smiling, cooing, and showing less tension in his body.

2. Describe a time when you engaged in reflection on a caregiving/teaching practice. Discuss how you changed your behavior.

In this section of the chapter, the authors will assist you in examining the use of two tools, dialogue and reflection, in the resolution of value conflicts between the personal/professional self and the NAEYC Code values. You will read an example of this type of conflict between personal/professional values and the values expressed by the NAEYC Code. You will also see how the tools of dialogue and reflection can help in reconciling the conflict.

In the following scenario you will see a conflict between the personal/professional self and an NAEYC Code value. Stephanie, age 16, and Juan, age 18, are parents of Emma Joy, age two months. Emma Joy is enrolled in the high school child care center while Stephanie and Juan attend classes. Stephanie proudly tells Maria, the caregiver/teacher with sixteen years of experience and a master's degree in early care and education, that every weekend she and Juan take Emma Joy to the high school football game. Maria thinks that Emma Joy is too young to sit in the cold in a large crowd at a football game. After all, when she was raising her children, she did not take them out until they were older and her mom did not take her out as an infant. Maria decided to consult with her colleague, Dee, about her concerns. Dee asked Maria questions about the situation and reminded her about the NAEYC Code value that states a commitment to "appreciating and supporting the close ties between the child and family." Dee suggested that Maria talk about her concerns with Stephanie and Juan. After learning from Stephanie and Juan that Emma Joy was dressed appropriately, Maria reflected on her own attitude and her discussion with Dee. Knowing that Emma Joy was dressed appropriately, was spending enjoyable time with both parents, and could continue to be nursed by her mom, Maria realized that there were some benefits to Emma Joy in this family outing. The next time Stephanie told Maria that she and Juan were taking Emma Joy to the game, Maria said, "What a great idea. I am so glad that you are spending family time together."

What we are seeing in this scenario is a conflict between Maria's personal/professional self and the NAEYC Code. Maria's personal self informs her that infants should not be taken to football games. Her value is supported by her home values, that is, "my mother never would have taken us as infants to football games and I did not take my own children as infants to football games." Maria's professional self is also in conflict with the NAEYC Code core value in that her professional training in health and safety issues related to infant caregiving supports her professional self idea that infants should not be out in the cold at football games. Both Maria's personal and professional self are in conflict with the NAEYC Code value that supports close ties between the child and family. What moved Maria from her personal/professional values to the NAEYC Code value was dialogue and reflection with her colleague, Dee.

At this point in our discussion, we will discuss the two tools, dialogue and reflection, that can help to reconcile conflict between the personal/professional self and the values of the NAEYC Code. We will use the example of Maria to provide greater clarity in the discussion of dialogue and reflection. Dialogue occurs when two individuals come together and have a conversation about their differing values for the purpose of understanding from where those values came. The reconciliation of Maria's personal/professional values that conflicted with the NAEYC core values began when she entered into dialogue with her colleague, Dee. Prior to Maria thinking that taking Emma Joy to the football game was a great idea, Maria held the personal value that an infant should not be taken to football games. Her personal value was supported by her upbringing and her thinking that she was a more mature mother than Stephanie. After all, she was twenty-six when she had her first baby and thought she was mature enough to know that infants should not be in the environment of a football game. Maria's professional values were also in conflict, given that she has had formal training in health and safety issues related to infant caregiving. She had been reminded by her training that caregivers should inform parents of preventive health measures that support the well-being of the child. She believed that she should tell Stephanie and Juan that taking an infant out in the cold is not beneficial to the infant.

In addition to the tool of dialogue, reflection is a useful tool for resolving conflicts. Reflection occurs when an individual during the dialogue pauses to examine how his/her assumptions and values affect both thinking and behavior. The dialogue and reflection processes support the necessary thinking to change behavior. We can see from the example of Maria and Stephanie how the tools of dialogue and reflection can help us when personal/professional values conflict with the NAEYC Code values.

To further explain the use of dialogue and reflection to resolve conflicts, let us go back to our scenario. As you remember, Maria was concerned about Stephanie and Juan taking their young baby to a football game. Maria entered into a dialogue with her colleague, Dee. She shared with Dee her concerns about the inappropriateness of Emma Joy attending the football games because of the cold weather and being in a crowd of people. She also mentioned to Dee that she has been an infant teacher for the past sixteen years, has been a parent, and has had formal training in infant/toddler care. Dee then asked Maria to think even more deeply about her values and beliefs and asked Maria about how her mother would have responded to this situation. Maria says that her mom never would have taken her to a football game as an infant and would have told her never to take her child to a football game at such a young age.

To help Maria gain more clarity in understanding her conflict, Dee shared with Maria that she had taken her infants to football games well dressed and there had been no ill effects. In fact, the outing had strengthened their family's relationship. Dee's information supported Maria in thinking more deeply about the values that were driving her concern. Dee also invited Maria to think about the NAEYC Code. She reminded her that one of the values of the Code is appreciating and supporting the close ties between child and family. Maria then told Dee that she really believes in appreciating and supporting the close ties between the child and family.

Thus, we see the power of dialogue between Maria and her colleague Dee. They had a rich conversation but also took a deeper look at the issues and challenged assumptions or "common sense" notions. Dialogue enables people to closely examine their values, assumptions, and behaviors. Dialogue enables people to become aware of how their values impact their behaviors and how those values may conflict with other values, in this case, the NAEYC Code value. In reviewing their conversation, we can see how Maria, with Dee's help, begins to reflect. Brookfield (1995) suggests that "talking to colleagues about problems we have in common and gaining their perspectives on these increases our chances of stumbling across an interpretation that fits what is happening in a particular situation" (p. 36).

What Maria learns is that her conflict is between her personal/professional values and the values of the NAEYC Code. Dee's invitation to Maria to think about her values, both personal and professional, challenged Maria to reflect on the conflict. The reflection process enabled Maria to gain insight into why she wanted to tell Stephanie and Juan to refrain from taking their baby to the game. What she learned was that her way of thinking wasn't the only way of thinking about this issue. Her dialogue with Dee enabled her to have the courage to say to Stephanie and Juan, "What a great idea! I am so glad that you are spending family time together," because she examined through dialogue and reflection her personal/professional values and the NAEYC Code values. Maria's reflection of the experiences, assumptions, attitudes, and values supporting her previous thinking moved her to a new way of thinking and a new behavior that reconciled her conflict. According to Brookfield (1995), without the habit of reflection, "we run the continual risk of making poor decisions and bad judgments. We take actions on the basis of assumptions that are unexamined." We fall into habits of justifying what we do by reference to unchecked common sense "and of thinking that the unconfirmed evidence of our own eyes is always accurate and valid" (pp. 3–4).

We have explored Maria's conflict between her personal/professional values and the values of the NAEYC Code. Maria had a choice to maintain her current position, that is, suggest to the young parents that they keep their infant at home, or move to another position, that is, affirming the parents' decision and describing the benefit. Maria learned that utilizing the tools of dialogue and reflection gave her necessary information and insight to reconcile the conflicting values.

What I Have Learned

Reflective Questions

If you are in a classroom setting, "Think, Pair, and Share." Think about your response to the question, find a partner, and share your responses. If you are not in a classroom setting, share your thinking with a friend.

1. What have you learned about the concept of personal/professional self?
2. What excites you about the tools of dialogue and reflection?
3. Why do you think it is important to learn to use the tools of dialogue and reflection in your work as an early care and education practitioner?
4. Create a scenario in which an early care and education practitioner has a conflict between the personal/professional self and the NAEYC Code. Describe how the tools of dialogue and reflection will benefit the practitioner in this situation.

CELEBRATING OUR UNDERSTANDING

In the first section of this chapter you analyzed the relationship between the personal/professional self and the core values of the NAEYC Code. In the final section of this chapter you examined the tools of dialogue and reflection. You engaged in reading about how the tools of dialogue and reflection facilitated by a colleague can assist the practitioner in resolving conflicts between personal/professional self and core values of the profession. What is exciting is knowing that as a practitioner you have tools available to you to use when value conflicts occur. These tools can help you feel confident in the workplace. As a practitioner you need to feel confident in your professional judgment in order to ensure quality services for young children and their families.

Give yourself a hug for finishing this chapter and join us in the next chapter, where you will use a review process to analyze and resolve ethical dilemmas.

RESOURCES AND REFERENCES

Bourdieu, P., & Passeron, J. (1991). *Language and symbolic power.* Cambridge, MA: Harvard University Press.

Brookfield, S. D. (1995). *Becoming a critically reflective teacher.* San Francisco, CA: Jossey-Bass.

Vella, J. (1995). *Training through dialogue: Promoting effective learning with adults.* San Francisco, CA: Jossey-Bass.

Chapter 3

USING OUR UNDERSTANDING OF THE NAEYC CODE AND A REVIEW PROCESS TO ANALYZE AND RESOLVE ETHICAL DILEMMAS

In the previous chapters you have learned about the NAEYC Code, your personal/professional relationship to the NAEYC Code and the use of the tools of dialogue and reflection. In this chapter you will learn about a review process that can assist you in your daily challenges with ethical dilemmas. Nash (1996) suggests that ethical dilemmas are complex in nature and require consideration of several factors including "the act, the intention, the circumstances, the principles, the beliefs, the outcomes, the virtues, the narrative, the community, and the political structures" (p. 20). Brophy-Herb, Kostelnik, and Stein (2001) remind us that a review process is needed because "ethical issues usually are ambiguous with no clear course of action readily apparent" (p. 82). A review process provides practitioners with guidelines for dealing with the ambiguities of ethical issues and/or dilemmas.

The suggested review process for analyzing and resolving ethical dilemmas consists of five stages: (1) apply to the situation a consistent definition of ethical dilemma; (2) use knowledge of the NAEYC Code of Ethical Conduct to guide personal/professional self-reflection and dialogue and reflection with a colleague; (3) exercise and act on an ethical judgment; (4) reflect on the ethical judgment and explore opportunities for professional change; and (5) facilitate professional change. As a practitioner it is important for you to know this review process so that you can analyze and resolve ethical dilemmas that you encounter in your workplace. In this chapter, you will learn about and practice using the review process for analyzing and resolving ethical dilemmas by examining and responding to scenarios with ethical dilemmas.

As you engage in the reading and activities in this chapter, you will have an opportunity to identify what you already know about ethical dilemmas. You will also synthesize what you have learned in each section of the chapter and celebrate your understanding of the NAEYC Code and a review process to analyze and resolve ethical dilemmas.

Knowledge about the NAEYC Code and review process will assist you in your professional journey as you encounter complex ethical dilemmas.

GUIDING IDEAS

- Practitioners can use the NAEYC Code and a review process to analyze and resolve ethical dilemmas that they encounter in the workplace.
- Practitioners can use scenarios to practice using the NAEYC Code and a review process to resolve ethical dilemmas.

ACHIEVEMENT-BASED OBJECTIVES

Through reading, engagement, and reflection, learners will have:

- Explored a review process that can be used to analyze and resolve ethical dilemmas in the workplace.
- Practiced using the NAEYC Code and a review process to analyze and resolve ethical dilemmas.

EXPLORING THE REVIEW PROCESS

 What I Know Activity

Please read the following scenarios and identify each one as an ethical responsibility (ER) or an ethical dilemma (ED)

_____ 1. Mrs. Huerta, Lucas's mother, has brought to your class a birthday cake, candy, cookies, and soft drinks to celebrate Lucas's birthday. Mrs. Huerta could leave her workplace only at 11:00 A.M., that is, one hour before the children's regular lunchtime. Mrs. Huerta wants you to serve the birthday snack when she is in the classroom.

_____2. Jacob has been in time out for fifteen minutes because he did not stay in line when he was going to the cafeteria with his class. You question your teacher assistant as to why Jacob has been in time out for such a long period. Your teacher assistant tells you that the reason that Jacob has been in extended time out is that he obviously had not learned that it was not O.K. to get out of line. The teacher assistant really believes that Jacob will come to understand that his behavior has to change as a result of extended time out. She adamantly tells you that the goal is self-regulation.

1. Explain why you identified #1 as either an ethical responsibility or an ethical dilemma.
2. Explain why you identified #2 as either an ethical responsibility or an ethical dilemma.

The review process, consisting of five stages, assists practitioners in analyzing and resolving ethical dilemmas. In this section of the chapter, we will explore the five stages of the review process.

A Five-Stage Review Process for Resolving Ethical Dilemmas

1. **Apply to the situation a consistent definition of ethical dilemma.**
2. Use knowledge of the NAEYC Code of Ethical Conduct to guide personal/professional self-reflection and dialogue and reflection with a colleague.
3. Exercise and act on an ethical judgment.
4. Reflect on the ethical judgment and explore opportunities for professional change.
5. Facilitate professional change.

The practitioner in the first stage of the review process uses a consistent definition to determine whether a situation constitutes an ethical issue. Every day in practice you encounter challenging situations that have an ethical component. According to Nash (1996), an ethical issue involves questions of morality, right or wrong, and responsibility. Ethical issues address human well-being or what is in the best interests of those individuals with whom we work. The situation may be related to your work with children, families, colleagues, and the community and society. Once a practitioner decides whether the issue has ethical considerations, he or she must next decide whether the situation involves an ethical responsibility or an ethical dilemma.

In the NAEYC Code, ethical responsibilities or standards of behavior agreed upon by the early care and education profession are identified for each group of individuals with whom a teacher works: children, families, colleagues, and the community and society. An ethical responsibility guides the behavior of practitioners. For example, an ethical responsibility to children is: "**We shall not participate in practices that discriminate against children by denying benefits, giving special advantages, or excluding them from programs or activities on the basis of their race, ethnicity, religion, sex, national origin, language, ability, or the status, behavior, or beliefs of their parents.**" From this NAEYC Code statement of ethical responsibility, we can see expectations for practitioner behavior supported by the professional knowledge base. Ethical responsibilities provide guidance to the practitioner but do not give specific solutions to conflicts. For instance, if Tomas hits Andrew over the head with a block, you will not find in the NAEYC Code either the words or actions you might use to handle this situation. What you will find are the general guiding principles that can support your decision making. The ethical responsibility in the NAEYC Code that supports decision making in this case is, "Our paramount responsibility is to provide safe, healthy, nurturing, and responsive settings for children" (Section I, NAEYC Code). In this statement one finds guidance rather than suggestions for specific actions.

Sometimes we encounter complex issues that have a moral component and possible costs and benefits to individuals. Such complex issues are called ethical dilemmas. Feeney and Freeman (1999) define an ethical dilemma as "a situation an individual encounters in the workplace for which there is more than one possible solution, each carrying a strong moral justification" (p. 24). Also, according to Feeney and Freeman (1999), "A dilemma requires a person to choose between two alternatives each of which has some benefits but also some costs" (p. 24). An ethical dilemma exists when core values from the NAEYC Code are in conflict. The core values represent the agreed upon morality of the profession that provides the practitioner with an idea of professional right and wrong.

To further explain the definition of ethical dilemma, we will provide a scenario. The mother of a three-year old has asked you, the teacher, not to give her daughter a snack in the afternoon because it interferes with dinner. The mom has to give her daughter an early dinner so that she can get to her evening work shift on time. You have observed that the child is hungry at snack time. What we can see from this scenario is: (1) there is more than one possible solution; (2) the practitioner must choose between two alternative responses, both of which have costs and benefits; and (3) there is a conflict between NAEYC core values. The alternative responses might be to give the child a snack in the afternoon to meet the child's needs or to honor the request of the mom. The teacher believes that not feeding the child when hungry is wrong; however, she also believes that not respecting the requests of parents is wrong. In this situation there are costs and benefits for the mom, the child, and the teacher in each possible response. Ethical dilemmas stem from conflicts with the core values of the NAEYC Code. In this scenario, the core value that is being challenged is: **"Helping children and adults achieve their full potential in the context of relationships that are based on trust, respect, and positive regard."** When the teacher asks herself if the conflict has to do with right and wrong, then we can conclude that there is an ethical dilemma. It is an ethical dilemma because there are two different ways of resolving this issue. Each possible resolution has benefits and costs. For example, if the teacher feeds the child, the mother will be unhappy because her request was not honored, her schedule will be interfered with, and she may consider moving her child to another program. If, on the other hand, the teacher honors the request of the mom, the child might be fussy and tired and unable to fully participate in planned activities because her hunger needs are not met. Finding a resolution to ethical dilemmas requires practitioners to understand that one core value is being challenged by another core value and that there are alternative responses that have elements of morality and costs and benefits tied to it.

By using a consistent definition of ethical dilemma, practitioners know whether or not a situation is an ethical responsibility or an ethical dilemma. If the situation is determined to be an ethical responsibility, the practitioner exercises professional judgment as prescribed by the ethical responsibilities stated in the NAEYC Code. If the situation is deemed an ethical dilemma, the practitioner continues the review process.

A Five-Stage Review Process for Resolving Ethical Dilemmas

1. Apply to the situation a consistent definition of ethical conduct.
2. **Use knowledge of the NAEYC Code of Ethical Conduct to guide personal/professional self-reflection and dialogue and reflection with a colleague.**
3. Exercise and act on an ethical judgment.
4. Reflect on the ethical judgment and explore opportunities for professional change.
5. Facilitate professional change.

The second stage of the review process is to use knowledge of the NAEYC Code to guide personal/professional self-reflection and dialogue and reflection with a colleague. Early care and education practitioners must have knowledge of the NAEYC Code as a framework to guide the analysis and resolution of ethical dilemmas. A practitioner can gain knowledge of the NAEYC Code by accessing the code in a variety of places including, but not limited to, Chapter 1 of this book; Feeney and Freeman's book, *Ethics and the Early Childhood Educator: Using the NAEYC Code;* the NAEYC website, www. naeyc.org; NAEYC brochures, local training and technical assistance and/or child care resource and referral programs. The practitioner then uses his or her knowledge of the Code to guide his or her personal/professional reflection and dialogue with colleagues. Reflection and dialogue, as discussed in Chapter 2, are important tools in the review process to guide the practitioner into clarity of thought about right and wrong as agreed upon by the profession in the NAEYC Code and costs and benefits related to the ethical dilemma.

To illustrate the second stage of the review process, we would like to revisit the second scenario in the What I Know Activity at the beginning of this chapter. If you remember, five-year-old Jacob has been in time out for fifteen minutes because he did not want or was not able to stay in line when going to the cafeteria with his class. The teacher in Jacob's classroom questions the assistant teacher about her method of addressing Jacob's behavior. As she reviewed the situation, she applied the agreed-upon definition of ethical dilemma to determine whether this was an ethical responsibility or an ethical dilemma. She consulted the NAEYC Code and recognized a conflict of core values: **"basing our** work with children on knowledge of child development" and "respecting the dignity, worth, and uniqueness of each individual (child, family member, and colleague)" (core values). The teacher concluded that because there was a conflict of core values, whose resolution would have both benefits and costs to the assistant teacher and the child, there was definitely an ethical dilemma. We can see that the teacher accessed the NAEYC Code to specify the conflicting core values. Once the teacher identified the core values, she acts on her knowledge of the NAEYC Code by engaging in personal/professional self-reflection and finding a colleague with whom to enter into collegial dialogue and reflection. We will now demonstrate how this is done.

Let us review our dilemma. The assistant teacher puts Jacob in time out for fifteen minutes because he did not stay in line when going to the cafeteria with his class. The classroom teacher believes that this is not an appropriate manner in which to address Jacob's behavior. The teacher then consults the NAEYC Code and specifies the conflicting core value: "basing our work with children on knowledge of child development" and "respecting the dignity, worth, and uniqueness of each individual." The teacher engages in personal/professional self-reflection. She reviews her personal values as well as her interpretation of professional values and standards of the profession. The teacher seeks out a colleague who could be the center director, a member of her or his professional organization, or other professional colleague. The teacher enters into a dialogue with her colleague, the classroom teacher in the next room. Brophy-Herb, Kostelnik, and Stein (2001) tell us that according to Nash (1996), "Providing opportunities for practitioners to talk about the basis of their actions may help novices understand and appreciate differences in judgment even when they do not agree with positions different from their own" (p. 82). The teacher explains to her colleague her reference to the NAEYC Code and selection of the core values that she believes relate to the dilemma. Her colleague asks her to delineate the costs and benefits of her possible responses. There are costs and benefits to the child and to the teacher assistant. Her colleague then reflects to the teacher what she has heard in order to assist the teacher in gaining further knowledge about the situation. The colleague encourages the teacher to engage in personal/professional reflection and its relationship to the core values in conflict. Some questions the colleague might ask the teacher during the dialogue to help the teacher clarify her thoughts and feelings might include:

- What are you going to do?
- How do you feel about what you are going to do?
- Why is it important that you address this situation?
- What are you going to do next? (Spencer, 1989)

The teacher responded by saying that what she did was: (1) look at the NAEYC Code; (2) use her professional knowledge base; and (3) review her personal values related to this situation. She stated that she was worried about her relationship with the teacher assistant. For her, the importance in addressing this dilemma was that it has implications for the child, for the teacher, and for the teacher assistant as well as for professional change, i.e. in-service training. She stated that the action she will take is to invite the teacher assistant to join her in the comfortable staff lounge to talk about her choice of guidance strategies.

Of course, the ideal is to reflect and dialogue with a colleague. However, we know in reality, often an ethical dilemma requires an immediate resolution. In this event, the practitioner would use the four questions indicated above to reflect on the dilemma and then act on his/her decision. After the resolution of the dilemma, the practitioner might then seek out a colleague to further reflect on the resolution. We have seen in the second stage of the review process how the practitioner engages in dialogue and personal/professional reflection to gain information about the situation. This information positions the practitioner to move into Stage 3 of the review process.

A Five-Stage Review Process for Resolving Ethical Dilemmas

1. Apply to the situation a consistent definition of ethical dilemma.
2. Use knowledge of the NAEYC Code of Ethical Conduct to guide personal/professional self-reflection and dialogue and reflection with a colleague.
3. **Exercise and act on an ethical judgment.**
4. Reflect on the ethical judgement and explore opportunities for professional change.
5. Facilitate professional change.

The third stage of the review process invites the practitioner to exercise and act on an ethical judgment. Ethical judgment refers to the reflection of the practitioner on the information collected from the dialogue and personal/professional reflection. Once the ethical judgment is made, the practitioner reflects on the information that has been gathered and the practitioner acts on his or her knowledge. It is the practitioner's courage for resolving the dilemma that transforms knowledge to action. This movement from knowledge to action also encompasses the acts of caring and creative thinking.

In the case described above, the teacher knew that she had to take an action based on the information she had collected. She thought about how she is going to approach the teacher assistant with her concern for the teacher assistant's guidance technique with Jacob. Her actual conferencing with the teacher assistant is the demonstration of her movement from knowledge to action through courage, caring, and creative thinking. In this scenario, she acts on her decision by entering into dialogue with the teacher assistant. She asks the teacher assistant why she chose "time out" as a response to Jacob's behavior. The teacher invites the teacher assistant to explore her position from both a personal and professional perspective. The teacher asks questions that help the teacher assistant to reflect on her actions. The teacher then proceeds to share with the teacher assistant that she has a dilemma because she is in disagreement with the teacher assistant's choice of action with Jacob.

The teacher and teacher assistant dialogue about their differing opinions and values regarding guidance techniques and work toward reaching agreement. For this example, the teacher's entering into dialogue with the teacher assistant facilitated an agreement. Through this dialogue the teacher assistant became aware of the personal/professional values that influenced her decision to put Jacob in time out for fifteen minutes. The dialogue provided clarity for her that caused her to rethink her guidance technique. She was able to assess the costs and benefits for the child and decided that it was worth a try to embrace another guidance method. The teacher assistant realized that by not talking to Jacob about his behavior and placing him away from his peers for such an extended period of time she was putting him at risk for lowered self-esteem and no behavioral change. The teacher's suggestion that she engage the child in problem solving seemed to provide more benefits to the child by helping him to understand his choice of behavior. In fact, according to Reynolds (1996), using the problem-solving method enhances a child's self-esteem as he masters social and problem-solving skills. Once the practitioner exercises professional judgment and acts on a decision, he or she moves into the fourth stage of the review process.

A Five-Stage Review Process for Resolving Ethical Dilemmas

1. Apply to the situation a consistent definition of ethical dilemma.
2. Use knowledge of the NAEYC Code of Ethical Conduct to guide personal/ professional self-reflection and dialogue and reflection with a colleague.
3. Exercise and act on an ethical judgment.
4. **Reflect on the ethical judgment and explore opportunities for professional change.**
5. Facilitate professional change.

The fourth stage of the review process is the practitioner's reflection on the exercised ethical judgment and exploration of opportunities for professional change. Professional change refers to action that the practitioner will take to revise or modify an existing policy or practice. The ethical dilemma is the catalyst for identifying the policies or practices that enabled the initial ethical dilemma. In this stage the practitioner again conducts a self-talk that includes the questions: What did I do? How did I feel about it? Why was it important that I did what I did? What policy or practice that supported the ethical dilemma needs to be changed? The practitioner's reflection in this stage has two purposes: (1) to reconcile and act on personal thoughts, feelings, or concerns related to the ethical dilemma, and (2) to provide information to move to the last stage of the review process.

The reconciliation can lead to follow-up activities, specific to the ethical dilemma. For example, the teacher might want to act on her personal reflection by touching base with the teacher assistant to ensure that there is no misunderstanding and that the teacher assistant has followed up with the agreed-upon resolution strategy. The intent of the reconciliation is to safeguard the practitioner's personal/professional relationship. The first purpose can also provide an opportunity for the teacher to evaluate the appropriateness and effectiveness of the resolution of the dilemma. For example, if talking to the teacher assistant does not produce changed behavior, then the teacher will need to seek an alternative strategy. The second purpose of this reflection provides the practitioner with information needed to move into the final stage of the review process, that of creating professional change. It may be that the larger system needs to be reviewed, and the ethical dilemma red-flagged that need.

A Five-Stage Review Process for Resolving Ethical Dilemmas

1. Apply to the situation a consistent definition of ethical dilemma.
2. Use knowledge of the NAEYC Code of Ethical Conduct to guide personal/professional self-reflection and dialogue and reflection with a colleague.
3. Exercise and act on an ethical judgment.
4. Reflect on the ethical judgment and explore opportunities for professional change.
5. **Facilitate professional change.**

In the final stage of the review process, the practitioner looks at the bigger context in which the ethical dilemma occurred. In the scenario above, the bigger context is professional development. The other stages in the review process provide the practitioner with a variety of information that can be useful in determining the center policies and practices that are in need of change. For example, the ethical dilemma described above led the teacher to clearly understand that there is a need to review the in-service training component for teacher assistants. It seems that her teacher assistant lacked a current knowledge of the use of appropriate guidance techniques. The in-service training structure might be reviewed, e.g. to look at a system of follow-up and feedback.

The review process for the resolution of ethical dilemmas not only may address the ethical dilemma but also may pinpoint areas for improvement related to personnel, program procedures, curriculum, or other aspects of an early care and education program. The review process takes the practitioner on a journey that helps the practitioner identify and resolve the dilemma and move toward professional change. Practitioners using the review process can gain valuable information to promote quality in early care and education programs.

What I Have Learned

Reflective Questions

Reflective Questions

If you are in a classroom setting, think, pair, and share. Think about your responses to the questions/statement. Find a partner and share your responses. If you are not in a classroom setting, share your thinking with a friend.
  1. What did you learn about the review process?
  2. Why is each stage of the review process important?
  3. What stage in the review process do you think will be most difficult for you and why?
  4. Why is it important to use ethical dilemmas to facilitate professional change?

USING SCENARIOS TO PRACTICE THE REVIEW PROCESS

What I Know Activity

1. List the five stages of the review process.
2. Differentiate between an ethical responsibility and an ethical dilemma.

3. Describe the use of the tools of dialogue and reflection in the review process.

In this section of the chapter, you will read a scenario and walk through the review process with the authors. The scenario will represent a complex ethical issue that an early care and education practitioner might encounter in his or her work. The authors will apply the five steps of the review process to this scenario through a dialogue. We will need to remind ourselves that there are not always easy answers and that the review process may cause discomfort. Ethical dilemmas require resolution through the use of courage, caring and creative thinking.

Scenario

You are an employee in a child care center. Your director announces at a staff meeting that beginning in a month, the center will be offering child care services on a 24-hour-per-day, 7-day-a-week schedule. She also announced that there would be three shifts to cover the 24-hour periods. Shift #1 is from 6:00 A.M. to 2:00 P.M. Shift #2 is from 2:00 P.M. to 10:00 P.M. Shift #3 is from 10:00 P.M. to 6:00 A.M. Currently there are nine children, two infants, four toddlers, and three preschoolers who will need 36-hour, around-the-clock care because of their moms' shifts at the hospital. They will be dropped off at 6:00 A.M. on Monday and picked up at 6:00 P.M. on Tuesday. You have been asked by the director to work shift #3 from 10:00 P.M. Monday to 6:00 A.M. Tuesday and shift #2 from 2:00 P.M. until 10:00 P.M. on Tuesday.

The authors have selected this scenario, which highlights the "marked changes in the nature, schedule and amount of work engaged in by parents of young children" (National Research Council and Institute of Medicine, 2000, p. 2), to demonstrate the use of the review process to resolve the ethical dilemma. The first step of the review process asks us to apply a consistent definition to determine whether the situation is an ethical responsibility or an ethical dilemma. Feeney and Freeman's (1999) definition includes the following components: (1) more than one possible solution; (2) a choice between two alternatives, each of which have some benefits and some costs; and (3) a conflict between two core values. She sees that there are two alternatives available to her. She can remain as an employee and work the shifts requested by her director despite the fact that she believes that it is wrong for children to be out of home in center care around the clock. Or she can resign and find employment in a child care program that provides traditional hour out-of-home child care because she believes that round-the-clock out-of-home child care does not support the developmental needs of children. In this scenario, for the practitioner the core values in conflict are: "**Basing our work with children on knowledge of child development**" and "**Recognizing that children are best understood and supported in the context of family, culture, community, and society.**" These core values are in conflict for the practitioner because she believes that there is nothing in the knowledge base of child development that supports round-the-clock out-of-home center care for young children. She also read the current research, which states "The consequences of the changing context of parental employment for young children are likely to hinge on how it affects the parenting they receive and the quality of the caregiving they experience when they are not with their parents" (National Research Council and Institute of Medicine, 2000, p. 9*)*. The practitioner, at the same time, also realizes that children are best understood and supported in the context of family. In these families parents are required to work round-the-clock shifts in order to provide for their family. Centers providing family-friendly child care services understand that extending their service hours is the best way of responding to and supporting family child care needs. The practitioner's recognition that she has alternative choices, her understanding that the choices have costs and benefits, and the identification of the conflicting core values satisfy the requirements of the first stage of the review process.

Having satisfied the first stage of the review process, the authors will engage in an abbreviated personal/professional self-reflection and dialogue and reflect with each other as colleagues to review the second stage of the review process. Nancy will be the practitioner who has the dilemma. Luis-Vicente will be her colleague who is also employed as a teacher in the same center. That evening, Nancy consulted her copy of the NAEYC Code to clarify the core values that seemed to be in conflict. She entered the second stage of the review process (Use knowledge of the NAEYC Code of Ethical Conduct to guide personal/professional self-reflection and dialogue and reflection with a colleague) by engaging in personal/professional reflection. Personally, she believes that children should not be in group center care for more than eight hours per day.

Her experience is that she stayed home with her children while they were growing up because she valued family time together. Professionally she could not think of one workshop or professional reading that supported seven-day-a-week, twenty-four-hour center-based care. She also believes that because there are no professional preparation materials or training available to practitioners to guide them in this extended hour caregiving practice, it should not be available. The following morning, after tossing and turning for several hours during the night, she decided to enter into a dialogue with her colleague, Luis-Vicente. Over coffee with Luis-Vicente, she explained that she doesn't know if she can continue working in the center because she believes that she has an ethical dilemma regarding the new family-friendly work schedule. She told Luis-Vicente that she has consulted the NAEYC Code and has reflected personally and professionally on the conflicting values. Luis-Vicente asked her to clarify her personal/professional reflections, that is, why the values are so conflicting for her.

LV: "What did you find out about your personal values that contributes to the conflict?"
N: "As a mother of three, I would never leave my children in extended care. I don't think that children should be away from their families. It is just not right."
LV: "Do you think that all families think like this or can survive without additional child care services? Have you ever considered that some families think that this is just fine?"
N: "You are probably right. I hadn't thought that some families might think that this is just fine for children I have been too caught up personally to think 'out of the box.'"
LV: "What did you find out through your reflection about your professional self?"
N: "I just do not believe that based on our current knowledge of child development, children should be away from their families in center care when teachers are not professionally prepared to provide extended care."
LV: "Child care is an evolving practice and sometimes we find ourselves in situations that challenge our knowledge base. It seems that at this juncture the overriding need is to meet family needs and provide care according to their schedules. Meeting family needs on schedules that are different from traditional schedules is a signpost of our changing society."

N: "Although I heard what you said, I am still troubled with the concept of providing extended care. I worry about the detriments to children, staff, and family. I feel as if I need to resign and find another center with traditional hours, but I don't want to leave the director in a pinch and I am worried as to how long it will take to find other employment. My children need food on the table."

Luis-Vicente proceeded to engage Nancy in further reflection by asking her four reflective questions.

LV: "What are you going to do?"
N: "I just don't know. I feel so conflicted. I want to stand for my values but I am beginning to understand that as an early care and education practitioner I need to expand my thinking. I don't want to leave the children at the child care center; I like my director and the environment of the center. I need my salary to take care of my own family."

Luis-Vicente repeated the question: "What are you going to do?"

N: "I think I am going to try this new schedule. My children are older now and maybe I can adjust to a different time frame and still provide quality care. I will tell the director about my conflict."
LV: "It seems to me that you have gathered the sufficient information for you to make a decision even though it is a hard one."

LV: "How do you feel about what you are going to do?"
N: "I feel ambivalent and angry that I have to make this kind of choice. What are we doing to children and families!"

LV: "Why is it important that we dialogued about the ethical dilemma?"
N: "Yes, it was important and helpful to me that we dialogued."
LV: "Why was it important?"
N: "Because it really helped me to clarify the personal/professional conflicts that I had. I feel like I now have the courage, caring, and creative thinking to resolve this situation."

Then Luis-Vicente asked the last of the four questions, "What are you going to do next?"

N: "Despite how I feel about it, I am going to meet with my director and share my feelings. I will tell her that I will work the requested shifts but I will search for information about child care centers that offer family-friendly schedules."

From the four reflective questions that Luis-Vicente just asked, practitioners, in this case Nancy, can move into the third stage of the review process.

We can see that Nancy, with the help of her colleague Luis-Vicente, has resolved the ethical dilemma and is ready to exercise ethical judgment and act on her decision, the third stage of the review process. Exercising ethical judgment requires the practitioner to further reflect on the information collected from the personal/professional reflection and the dialogue. Nancy again thinks about her personal/professional self and makes the decision to remain in her place of employment and enter into dialogue with her director. She acts on her decision by thinking about how she is going to address her director with her concerns. She then proceeds to ask her director if she would have coffee with her to discuss her concerns about the new center schedule. Her actual conferencing with the director demonstrated her courage, caring, and creative thinking, which is the movement from knowledge to action. The fourth stage of the review process requires the practitioner to reflect on the ethical judgment and explore opportunities for professional change. That evening Nancy reflected on her conferencing with her director.

Nancy's reflection that evening identified opportunities for professional change in her center that demonstrated her movement into the fourth stage of the review process. She concluded that the issues of lack of professional preparation of staff for extended-hour center-based care continue to resurface. Her courage, caring, and creative thinking challenged her to make an appointment with her director to discuss this opportunity for professional change. The actual conferencing with her director about this change is the fifth stage of the review process, facilitating professional change.

The outcome of the conference with her director was a commitment on the part of the director to establish a relationship with the local university to explore and examine the implications of extended care for children and families. The director, too, believed that extended center-based care is a real challenge to the program and agreed to provide in-service training before the new shifts began.

What we have seen is the authors' use of the scenario to demonstrate the application of the five-stage review process. The review process for resolving ethical dilemmas takes a practitioner on a journey that is strategically designed to move the practitioner from the identification of the dilemma through the resolution of the dilemma. The process uses dialogue and reflection as tools to create the momentum necessary for professional change.

What I Have Learned

If you are in a classroom setting, think, pair, and share. Think about your response to the question, find a partner and share your response. If you are not in a classroom setting, share your thinking with a friend.

1. Review the scenario presented in the beginning of section 2 of this chapter.
2. What feelings emerged for you as a result of Nancy's dilemma?
3. Using the scenario, role-play with your partner or friend stage 2 of the review process (Use knowledge of the NAEYC Code of Ethical Conduct to guide personal/professional self-reflection and dialogue and reflection with a colleague). Debrief your role-play by comparing and contrasting your dialogue with that of the authors.
4. Think back to ethical dilemmas you have experienced in the past and describe how the five-stage review process might have helped you resolve the dilemmas.

CELEBRATING OUR UNDERSTANDING

In the first section of this chapter, you explored a review process to analyze and resolve an ethical dilemma. In the last section of this chapter, you practiced using the NAEYC Code and a review process to analyze and resolve ethical dilemmas. You learned that ethical dilemmas are complex in nature and do not have easy solutions. You also learned that the review process takes you on a journey that strategically moves you step by step toward the analysis and resolution of ethical dilemmas. You now have a process to guide you as you encounter in your workplace challenging ethical situations with children, families, colleagues, and community.

Now that you have completed reading and engaging with this book, do something nice for yourself!

RESOURCES AND REFERENCES

Brophy-Herb, H. E., Kostelnik, M. J., & Stein, L. C. (2001). A developmental approach to teaching about ethics using the NAEYC Code of Ethical Conduct. *Young Children, 1,* 80–84.

Feeney, S., & Freeman, N. (1999). *Ethics and the early childhood educator: Using the NAEYC Code.* Washington, DC: NAEYC.

Nash, R. (1996). *"Real world" ethics; Frameworks for educators and human service professionals.* New York: Teachers College Press.

National Research Council and Institute of Medicine (2000). *From neurons to neighborhoods: The science of early childhood development.* Committee on Integrating the Science of Early Childhood Development. Jack P. Shonkoff & Deborah A. Phillips, (Eds.) Board on Children, Youth, and Families, Commission on Behavioral and Social Sciences and Education. Washington, DC: National Academy Press.

Reynolds, M. (1996). *Guiding young children: A child centered approach* (2nd ed.). Mountain View, CA: Mayfield Publishing.

Spencer, L. (1989). *Winning through participation.* Dubuque, IA: Kendall Hunt.